landmark status woman: tanka sequences

Kati Mohr

Kati Mohr

landmark status woman

tanka sequences

Bibliographic information of the German National Library: The German National Library lists this publication in the German National Bibliography; detailed bibliographic data is available on the internet at http://dnb.dnb.de. The automated analysis of the work in order to obtain information, in particular about patterns, trends and correlations in accordance with §44b UrhG ("Text and Data Mining") is prohibited.

© 2024 Kati Mohr

Cover & illustrations: Kati Mohr

Published by BoD · Books on Demand GmbH
In de Tarpen 42, 22848 Norderstedt, Germany

Printed by Libri Plureos GmbH, Friedens-allee 273, 22763 Hamburg, Germany

ISBN: 978-3-7597-5208-6

To all my homes

contents

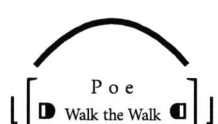

a few words, and then some more

Tanka are often written or translated in five lines in Western languages (but not solely), which gives a rough appearance of short, long, short, long, long. I don't always stick to this.

In my understanding of poetry (and art), a form does not only live by adhering to its number of lines, its rhythm, its line lengths and so on. There are other core components that are important and relevant to whether a poem can actually be called tanka, a poetic form that has existed in Japan for over a thousand years (including its predecessor waka). One of these, it seems to me, is the linking of observation, realisation and feeling within a concise poem. At a certain point in/between the lines, the brain switches to the heart. Others are the musicality and the use of great imagery.

I set out to read and explore a wider variety of tanka that are not exclusively written in five lines or/and have an amazing freshness and modernity, such as the tanka of Jun Fujita, Minosuke Noguchi, Kisaburo Konoshima, Machi Tawara,, Akitsu Ei, and Matsukaze.

Their powerful and moving tanka inspired me to push my writing further and use it to record my life, to preserve the emotions, but also to reflect them back to myself. Sometimes I can only recognise when I jot them down and reread.

What makes tanka so special? It is a very robust poem and at the same time open, otherwise it would not have been able to survive for so many years. It says: *It's okay, come to me and tell me where it hurts. Tell me why you're happy. Tell me your whole humanity, I will help you understand it.*

A multi-layered beauty, that's tanka for me.

This book combines traditional and modern themes, colloquial and literary language. Some tanka are concrete, vertical, written in one, two, three, four and five lines. They are arranged in sequences that aim to let each stanza shine in the company of its neighbours.

Whether you agree that every single tanka can actually be called a tanka is a moot question. The more important one (for me, and maybe for you as well) is: do they move you?

I sincerely hope they do.

PS. When one-line tanka run into the next line, I have indented those in order to distinguish them from two-line tanka. All illustrations in the middle of the book belong to a series called FRAMED | 2024.

in fact, quite the reverse should be true

in fact, quite the reverse should be true

it makes

no
sense

said every human

so

we
do
it

one drop of rain

after
the
other

blood-red sunset leaden down the road the house I grew up in

night after night a clouded roof I turn to f
a
n
c
y
w
o
r
k

the wind around the house
from room to room a pale and restless moon

the girl
gazes at
the stars
their silence is
maddening

mama blames her problems
on my efforts
to leave them behind
I still shut the door
by letting it slightly open

honour thy father and thy mother

at my feet

my
spirit   like a
  sparrow

whose feathers
move

nothing
more

I fall behind on the bumpy trail *he's just like my father* no *I'm just like*
  my mother

up close I see
the petals turning brown
the rose is still a rose
not the *what*
just the *how*

mama says
we're BEST friends
real girlfriends
under fields of clouds
there must be grass that one can touch

lilacs

stuck into

a bluish
tumbler

without water

I am not
myself

an uncaring woman, a bad woman
as much as I try, the milk is burnt into the hob

it isn't even
the amplitude . . .
in all cupboards on earth
I picture a bottle of wine

over and over
reading signs
on crossroads
as if I've never been
a swarm of swallows

an old cut in the crabapple bark
I feel akin
there's no cure.

jotting down
in my notes
a confession
to a priest
with earplugs

in my mind
these potholes
open wide
and everything becomes
the static of a river

I reach down to
the sink filled with water
on the surface
nothing changes
everything changes

a
trail
of
dried
up
orange
juice
on
the
kitchen
floor

the
heaviness

of
my
body

that
I want to

leave

behind

in fact, quite the reverse should be true

a bird flies up
close to my resting place
a warning
echoes
on the path

my thrumming chest
about to burst
a writhing, speechless dragon

a copter's search-and-rescue
in the dark
I wish they had been here for me

in a storm
the leaking window
talks
more to the body
than to the mind

yesterday they closed the street for maintenance
the badass I'm supposed to be is just trying to find a way home

walls
run around
a secret garden
I content myself
in dreams

in fact, quite the reverse should be true

the shape of a bird aims at the sun and disappears
of all options, this is the one I see

freezing in my spot
on the edge of the bed
the weight of the world
the same as mine

one cast-iron cup
and just enough of tea
I wish I could ease into
a cloudless sky

the dove on the sill, it looks me in the eye and flies
like anyone I open the window for

poetry . . .
can it save
the world, or me
is that even its job

end of *may*
it simply won't stop
raining . . .
as I love
I grieve

the sunshine's
dazzling gold
and yet I'm cold
it's hard to like
living among humans

I take my time walking home, in the pouring rain
at least there's nobody here who could drop a brick

the cedar in front of our house   in the rain   at dawn
a Sunday losing
                         its
                                 contour

a boy sneaks a peek on the rabbits in the carrier
I feel like crying, I don't know why

in fact, quite the reverse should be true

it's
fine

to grow

in just the right amount of sun and water

I
don't
miss

starving

from my sill a wild dove calls I am   here   I really am

triangle constructions

a
hazy
summer

of
two
years

we
thought

we
could

be
everything

we
cannot

the honk
of two geese
taking flight
it pulls
and pulls

with
nothing
else
to
do

than
being

anxious

there's
blood

under
my
fin
ger
nails

years of writing
poem after poem
didn't help
make him
no bully

it circles and circles in my head a plethora of heavy clouds

what's going on?
unable to find the words
I'm so upset
again not certain
about anything

coming into leaf too soon the first spring that frightens me

scribbling on the page right to the edge
I need to draw this line, no matter how well received

at the exit
on empty twigs
fake cherry blossoms
he quickly lets go
of my hand

polliwogs

in

my hands

he
thinks

I have betrayed

him

a coursing waterfall
it all comes out just wrong
the case close to some pseudonym control
why can't we stop it?

the slice into my heart is sharp and sudden
wait, I yell out, *please, I've wanted to tell you*
nothing comes out
nothing, really

I light the morning candle
all the birds don't
talk to me

his mindfuck I wish I could just wash off traces the intimacy what

he killed

in
me

the
slight
sweep

of a
black wing

the fairy lights above me darken one thought and then
   another fading

after I've taken the picture, I see it
the warm circle of sunshine on Nike

not for no reason
I hold a crushing rage
like parsley seeds
between his shadow
and mine

but I'm so furious
it makes me want to scream
I'm miserable
pumping in my veins
no blood

rather than
asking the stars
the way
ask yourself why
you need them to answer

hold it
isolate the sound
I close my eyes
the music stops
I can hear the blood river roar

all
anger

and now
there's something worse

the empty
house

morphing into

the empty
house

just look up
far into the sky
'cause that one's mine
a glance that holds months of feeling
like the worst person

an old ballroom
in lush blue, warm brown
the plafond with the scenes of gods
as damnable as us

the wind, the rain, the sun, the sandstone
that I can just rely on myself as long as I can

I can just sit around and grieve the time it needs to lift

driftwood . .
to swim alone against
the currents
wash me
to the empty shore

past frostbitten blossoms I'll keep coming back to *it was all my fault*

anything makes its way
briskly to the heart
early in my morning coffee:
prepositions

to even have these thoughts
go away, I think heartlessly
a hard shell
maybe I'm one now
I never was before

orchids
budding in winter
all at once
I shrink and call out
for my own buried grace

with one small step, the landscape shifts
so why not the mind, if that's all it takes?

sand
pulled out from under
the brittle willow
to bend and break and drift
elsewhere

the birds
stop to sing
I wake up
is it possible
not to lie to myself?

where you going?
the good old days
through the front door
so what do you do?
very good question

silhouetted
in the doorway
something fierce
I'm going to open
as I am

life [sic]

a new moon
the water lily blushes
colourless
I cannot stay in tune
of a sudden

songs & songs, Taylor
I know you know
I feather my bed
as so many others
in a magnifying glass

the dumpster
with ants
with soggy straw
flying from the lid

thrown shut

I really, really loved
the mornings
a car turns around
the corner
somewhere, somewhere

some will always
blame it on the willing
measure
the abyss between
us and fireflies

why cannot we say it
how it is
to cry 'cause life ...
a sea that calls
and bruises

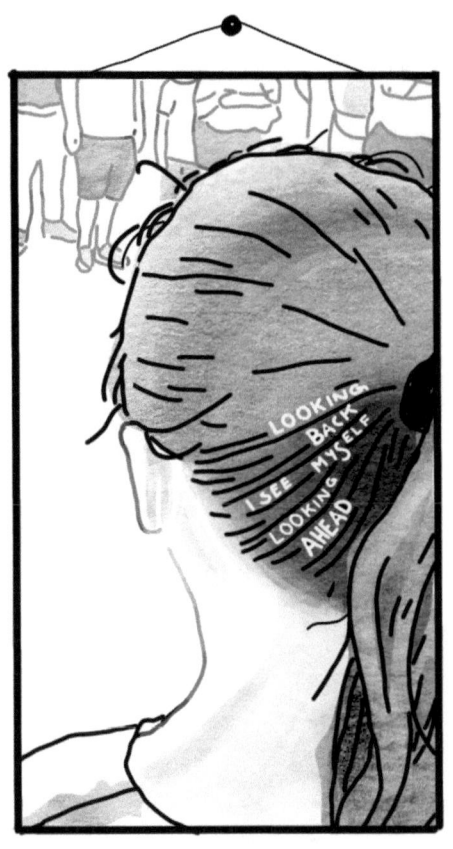

anything ever written has been written for the writer first

LIFE IS A STRETCH OF YEARS THAT BREAK CHARACTER

73

a house of making in a state of grace

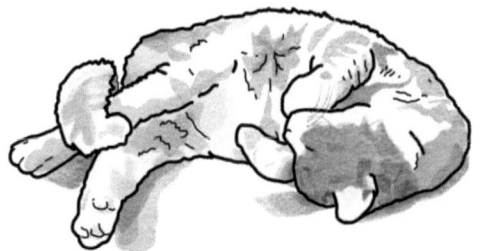

the spread of tarot cards between us
a rare moment of freedom
that I best myself and ask
can I come visit you again

      every house red bricks, white window frames
      we talk about the price we pay
      that our home should be
      where we feel at home

after breakfast many hours in the room with the piano I remember
    him playing the golden hour years ago

fresh sour dough bread in the basket
the better one, bought just for me
I joke around, so overwhelmed
that someone cares

I turn away
if not I'd say things no-one regrets
the half-eaten apple on the counter top

orange and yellow poppies
growing in my friends' front garden
this is just the way they are, delightfully happening

the cats duke it out
who's allowed to sleep in my bed
I have no say
except a *not at all*

down by the lake
a stranger tells us
swans are murderers
I decide to not take pictures
of the goslings

low ponding in the park
I wish I were a water skimmer
we walk back
the foreign suburb and two one-way streets

now that I'm so far away he texts what I've been waiting for so long

scones and sandwiches
I read the titles of the recipes aloud
let me be honest
I just hunger for connection

on a scale of counting all red things to not finding words
we settle at a table for bread and Boursin

behind the heavy curtains a dull, saturated morning mist
I put away what hurt too much, just put it last

reading matsukaze's tanka in my other home the wind turns and
    turns my idea of who I am now and who I have been then

we call it drizzle he says and I say that I meant my brain clotted
    cream

routines I learn for a week, to be unlearned later
spring flowers start to droop in the guest room

a soft sofa
with scratch marks and lose threads
up to the upper corner
I practise bearing
the quiet, my own unrest

one of the cats jumps on my legs
at 5:30 in the morning
purring like a machine
guess I'm adopted now

having breakfast
in a quiet house
I'm better
allowing myself to be not okay
among good friends

a cottage garden
with forget-me-nots
not estranged at all
I'm back! I'm back
as if I've never left

we plan activities
like baking scones, a movie, games, art gallery ...
during and after the cats

art installation of a city
they occupied
the everyday
unsettled
I sit down

among the beetles
pinned down on display
a doodling by *William, age six*
I'm stuck on
for this change of air

rooms with tools and tools with rooms overwhelmed by usefulness I
   wander among what makes us us

the mantis shrimp behind glass
once fierce
now faded and fragile
I too need protection

oil paintings of faces
peeling away any wish to please
I am strangely happy to comply

I study Joseph Wright's play of light for a long while
if I just had a final say in it, and I have[1]

---

[1] "Dear Human, I Don't Think Poets Are More Troubled Than Others", The Other
Bunny, September 2, 2024

to see with eyes unclouded by hate a story with no story and my
wholeness summoned

snacks after midnight
sweet and savoury
my languages meld
a happy, oblivious sloth

saying nothing at all, just watching each other rest
I caught a lost bee and let it fly into the morning

I find the letter 'B' on the pavement
keep it in my hand during our stroll
who knows its, indeed, who knows anybody's story

is it infectious?
all my unease gone
amidst such kindness
and foxes
and hares

sunk into the sofa
wrapped up in a blanket
I look closely at the painting of a forest
among the trees all kinds of autumn

now
that

my tears catch me off-guard

now
that

I become so quiet
I can just

please
and
thank you

what would you feel more comfortable with
a brief farewell or time together at the airport?
oh he knows, he knows me well
he lets me choose

it must be roofs and water that glisten so deep down below
I push my mind relentlessly to save his hug

back at home, I panic over the list of things to do
but he reminds me *let it begin with rest, self, treats*

landmark status woman

a table full of crumbs
that's how this day starts well enough

looking out over the infinite coffee in my mug
I've learned more than I realise

an old comment of mine liked by a stranger
and I cry, I laugh, this is it, this is my life

a soft cloth on my eyes I rest the mind yet dragonflies

in every direction
round a well-covered table
brilliant white clouds
I possess so much
then I feel sorry

how is it different?
the rain is pouring
the rain at night
telling me over and over again
to love this uncertain world

vivid greens, and here the grey geese lie
I try to stand out gracefully against myself

the trees lean in
flowers hold their petals still
you are a dreamer
as if nothing can go wrong
under this sky

where the moon should be knowing too much knowing too
little

what's in my future,
Cassandra? I ask
an ominous prophecy
as I go at a leisurely pace
letting my mind wander

I had to go
find secret messages, do things
but that's not it
a strange 1984 feel
and still harvesting

in a desert of concrete a sparrow gives me a nod and I nod back
just cracking on doing our thing, that's who we are

rain and rain and
croci and snowdrops
freshly cleaned
my bright white sneakers walk
in the shadow of it all

we have sex
and it's good
we have sex
and it's ... *fine*
time passed

the sudden burst
of liberated rain
I imagine
from inside the house
life is a parking lot

a full moon
every fibre in my body
telling me
existence becomes an act
in relative silence

I sit down to write
present tense, not past
our intercourse
everything smells
like salt

not having written much today
nothing makes sense
except that the dog hops
with each bark

an all grey day
of unexpected things
that drain
but it's okay —
I had broccoli for dinner

I've become
so accustomed
to perfection
all I hear is
lucky

the dryer's maintenance program
dropped from the manual
their hidden lies
contradict themselves

light and shadow
on the dirty glass
I watch them play
with my patience

as if
I heave

the wet laundry of many

lightly

they
keep
asking
why

I cannot work

invisible seeds
to which we have given names
come sit a little closer
as they will stretch themselves
you must see to it

reading to my mindful son the world at nighttime razor-thin

the rabbit's nose
pushed deep into the straw
I quietly say sorry
care can be a scary thing

hi, it's me of course
who should talk to our son
in confidence
how can I lose that weight
of being a woman

I make
my way across the lawn
part the curtain of leaves
the door swings open
part groan, part roar

the sparrows chirp wildly
in the overgrown garden
it's June again
with all that is thrown at me
what can I call mine?

        the roses
                go on a walk lately
          which is true
               I'm so fed up
       emotional all day

mild detergent
and compression tights—
doing the laundry
for a self
I yet have to grow into

wet snow on a spruce,
my tired tiredness—
is this just another state of being
a woman?

the real moon
well-rounded
full
all giving bodies
die in me

holding the cramped core of my body
how well trained it is to not show

I did not want him
to see me crying
and the stars came out
without saying anything
as usual

a figure unable to cry beside the river filling the fields, the houses —
    it takes a lot of rain

as our bodies part
my head must find
his heart
to hear its song thrush
come to rest

glows from behind the clouds
a full-time moon
I've written her down
to stay

I hear something
the sound trickles
closer
looking down at me
all my poems

I dreamt of writing the perfect poem one day
the dead mouth closed
with a skilful stitch through the lips
and a hidden knot

a canon of cornflowers whooshing past
how am I supposed to feel, to not feel this world?

never diving, but my feet on the railing

my face sinks into the cool, scooped water
the summer too much summer
we say it, but to no effect

the waves
a lush beat at the lake shore
us
smiling, not smiling
continually unalike

the blue sky, the blue water
we hold hands in the sun
briefly

we hop from swimming spot to swimming spot
I think I'll write a book about
connections

women in their bodies
and this is myself in mine:
I make it a — no, my problem

      beautiful, beautiful world
          I make a tally under my eyes
                 for every stretch mark

the sunlight dot-dot-dots the crests
just by thinking
I sweat

a sunset like any other
but more so
will this be our last?

with summer lightning
late at night
I'm lying in bed
writing, writing, writing

a door slams shut
but it doesn't need the door at all
it's a broken record, no matter how
you look at it

maybe we wrap the things up
we better just imagine, like kebabs
deep down a mystery

redoing all
the buttons on my blouse
speaking
my own truth

a naked toddler crawls into the grass
I can't help but wonder
what world do we leave?

never diving, but my feet on the railing

banana trees!
that makes me want to write
about Bashō...
but the obvious
never worked for me

my former friend's face
I'm content it's nowhere to be seen
in this charming old town
enough to rewire

I've slept well last night, finally
my yawn mingles with a bright ray of sun
through the bus window

my fingers play with the cowlick in my neck
this lazy day that just didn't want to end all week

coming back to the lake
to the same shaded bench
I zone in on the turquoise blue:
no place without humans

why am I crying, why?
it's just a book about loss and grief
and the infuriating smell of five courses

after the lashing rain
steaming pasta and leaf lettuce
in the dim kitchen
that's love, too

the rain in the riverbed
taking sides
I implore you
who will take mine?

in the bookstores
I target local authors—
my holiday home
with its white sliding door

the wet stain on the pillow
I must trace how often I choose
the easy way out

the weight of a stone that fits in my hand
almost disappearing
I reappear

thirteen swans
swimming, grooming, resting
I count the pages left

the profiles
of far-off mountains
our hands' shadow
held or meshed
it looks the same

am I numb, am I rational
to not worry
—they're swimming so far out

I sob, the audience laughs
life is absurd
backstage four hundred puppets dangle

never diving, but my feet on the railing

tomorrow, we'll travel home
it's so cliché
I think
of cherry blossoms

$about$ the author

K ati Mohr, born in 1976, is a German artist and poet, known online as pi & anne. She lives in Nuremberg with her family and two rabbits. Her aim is to explore the filters we humans use, because how we see things often says more about us than about the things themselves. She is still busy creating a collage of her own life that makes sense to her.

Her poems have appeared in a number of journals, e.g. Kingfisher Journal, The Haibun Journal, The Other Bunny, Whiptail Journal, The Pan Haiku Review, MacQueen's Quinterly.

She came second in the Marlene Mountain Memorial Contest 2023, organised by #FemkuMag. In 2024, her haibun "All These Things" was honoured with a Touchstone Award by The Haiku Foundation, and she released her first chapbook with tanka "something with feathers".

It's a pleasure to share my poetry with you, and if you have any questions, feel free to write to me :).

Here's some of the music I've listened to while writing.

Find more on *@pi.and.anne* and on *piandannes.wordpress.com*